Vitalizing the High School

A Curriculum Critique of Major Reform Proposals

by Gordon Cawelti

foreword by Glenys G. Unruh

Association for Supervision and Curriculum Development
1701 K Street, N.W., Suite 1100, Washington, D.C. 20006

Acknowledgments

Final editing of the manuscript and publication of this booklet were the responsibility of Robert R. Leeper, Associate Secretary and Editor, ASCD publications. Technical production was handled by Elsa Angell, with the assistance of Nancy Olson, Teola T. Jones, and Maureen Montgomery, with Caroline Grills as production manager.

Author

    Gordon Cawelti is Executive Director of the Association for Supervision and Curriculum Development. He served as Superintendent of Schools in Tulsa, Oklahoma, for four years prior to accepting his present position. His past positions include six years as high school principal and science teacher in Iowa, seven years as Executive Secretary of the Secondary Commission of the North Central Association of Colleges and Secondary Schools, and he has been a visiting lecturer at the Universities of Kansas, Colorado, Illinois, and Maryland. He received the degree of doctor of philosophy in curriculum from the State University of Iowa.

Contents

Foreword

Persons interested in secondary education, those concerned with the problems of the schools, and others involved with youth in seeking solutions to school-related problems, should find in this booklet far more than a collection of recommendations to educators. It is a useful document, not only because it brings together the recommendations of prestigious organizations concerned with secondary education, but also because of Gordon Cawelti's critique of the recommendations and synthesis of the whole.

It is interesting to note that all of these sets of recommendations were submitted to the public within the span of a year, centering around 1973. This very fact reveals the climate of concern surrounding secondary education today.

James B. Conant's *The American High School Today* is placed in its proper historical perspective in the introduction. Those of us who were around when Conant made his analysis of the nation's high schools now realize that his recommendations were modest. School board members, superintendents, and high school principals listened respectfully to him because Conant himself is a distinguished and notable person whose judgments are respected. Schools of the 1960's that were not meeting Conant's suggestions utilized his report to try to bring their staff and program "up to standard."

New dimensions enter into the five current sets of recommendations. These express awareness of the dissatisfactions of significant numbers of students with their high schools whether communicated through apathy or activism. The public, as well as students, is concerned but generally from a different viewpoint. Crisis writings by popular authors, demands for accountability by taxpayers, and expressions of dissatisfaction with schools in general and with high schools in particular provided inspiration for these sets of recommendations.

Worthy of note is the point that, although severe criticisms were leveled against the national curriculum projects of the 1960's for their "scholar" orientation and for the lack of participation in planning by teachers, students, parents, and school administrators, these recent panels and commissions also were made up largely of nonpractitioners. For the most part, teachers, students, and other immediate participants in the schools were omitted; however, at least one commission (the National Commission on the Reform of Secondary Education) made a serious effort to involve the grassroots participants in surveys and discussions to solicit their ideas. The collected recommendations bring to our attention the need for a sense of community—a united effort toward concerns for secondary education.

Cawelti's critique delineates very well the virtual absence of substantive curricular recommendations by the various panels, and notes the insufficient emphasis on the affective realm—the feelings and views of students.

Also, regardless of immediate problems, we must think of tomorrow, of what lies in the future. Futures research has brought to our attention the critical nature of curriculum decision making and the need for educators to give attention to our diminishing natural resources, overpopulation and starvation, a global view, and value clarification. Studies of the challenges of a postindustrial society which emphasizes humaneness and service seem appropriate if the developed nations are to move forward into a person-centered society and at the same time share expertise with underdeveloped nations so that they too can progress toward a society in which starvation and suffering are not a way of life.

Our challenge as curriculum workers is great. Let us not shirk by relying on simplistic solutions such as the dropping of compulsory education. We must remind ourselves that undeveloped countries have never had compulsory education; that education for all is one of the characteristics of an advanced society. Our challenge is to make education more relevant, humane, motivating, and, in some localities, more safe. Let us not retreat from our ideal of universal education but find new ways to plan learning environments in which choices are available, not only for our youth but for people of all ages. One thing is certain: we are living in a period of challenge and change in secondary education. The recommendations in this booklet must be seriously considered and acted upon, but even more is demanded of us. Therein lies our challenge as educators and curriculum workers.

GLENYS G. UNRUH
President, 1974-75
Association for Supervision and Curriculum Development
August 1974

1. Introduction

Almost 15 years have passed since James B. Conant issued his analysis of the nation's high schools, with recommendations for their improvement.[1] His report on secondary education, sponsored by the Carnegie Foundation, generated much interest among school people and citizens alike.

Since that time there has been apparent inactivity in this field until about 1973. In that year no less than a half dozen major reports were published, advocating substantial changes in the way American schools serve this age group. This ASCD booklet reviews the major recommendations of these six reports and affords a curriculum critique of their findings.

Conant's report was characterized as basically conservative. Nevertheless, many of us who were high school principals at the time can recall studiously reporting to our boards of education on what we were or were not doing in the light of his suggestions. His book, *The American High School Today*, was the "prestigious educator report" approach to curriculum making.

If Conant recommended that college-bound students have so many years of foreign language instruction, high schools often responded accordingly. He strongly affirmed America's belief in the comprehensive high school, thinking, perhaps naively, that if students from differing social classes got together for a course in Problems of Democracy, it would be instructive for all in seeking better understandings and relationships.

Like the much earlier Flexner report in medicine and medical education, the Conant report had great influence, but it was prob-

[1] James B. Conant. *The American High School Today.* New York: McGraw-Hill Book Company, 1959.

1

ably the last such individual study that will have so decided an effect on school practice. Although it is likely that the curriculum will never again be so greatly influenced by the report of a prestigious educator, the six reports from influential foundations and organizations that are reported herein well may set some major new directions for the high schools.

America's high schools are now graduating something like 80 percent of youngsters of secondary school age. Since so many young people are attending high school, why do these institutions need to be changed? What are the symptoms that indicate that the schools need to be reformed? The six major reports that are described herein have recurring observations which are pertinent to these questions.

1. The high holding power at present has made schooling the way of life for 14-17 year olds—it is much more socially undesirable not to attend high school than it was at the turn of the century.

2. Society thus provides a period of prolonged adolescence during which, it is contended, youths have little real involvement in worthwhile tasks through which they can develop a sense of responsibility.

3. Age segregation is a dominant pattern in our graded schools, thus denying high school youths interaction with younger or older persons.

4. The role of the home is less influential in helping young people move from schooling to work, and schools, it is contended, are doing much less than they should in combating unemployment and underemployment.

5. Students mature much earlier now than two or three decades ago but the curriculum has not yet recognized this; we underemphasize what young people can and should handle academically.

6. Schools have become increasingly impotent in reaching young people with formal instruction because of the power of competing influences such as the electronic media, travel, peer group influence, and work experiences.

Although the sixties saw widespread revolt against the non-responsiveness of high schools and colleges, campus life today is ostensibly more serene. There is some tendency among young people to seek self-fulfillment within the economic system rather than outside it—to tolerate a boring job so you can do the things you *really like* to do.[2]

There is little question about the extent of boredom in many of today's high schools. A comparison of student attitudes toward either innovative or traditional high schools supports this charge.[3] A sampling of seniors' views in both settings showed few differences. When asked how they felt about going to school each day, about a fifth of the seniors said that they ". . . very often dreaded the prospect of going to school each day," or "always disliked having to go to school." Moreover, half or more of the students in both innovative and traditional high schools were either indifferent or negative about the school environment, with boys significantly more dissatisfied than girls.

Throughout these reports one finds much concern for transition to the work world with experiential learning and work-study recommended. On this issue, there are some conflicting data. While such programs are repeatedly recommended, one study[4] which provided information from a questionnaire sampling of 16,409 high school seniors in 1972 showed slightly over three-fourths of them already working in paid or unpaid jobs.

High school enrollments are declining and will continue to do so for the next several years. This phenomenon is new for most schools. Some contend that American schools have always been coping with growth and enrollment quantities rather than with quality of program. Perhaps this decline will provide an opportunity to shift the focus. Schools may now be staffed with older and more experienced teachers thus necessitating more creative and supportive staff development programs.

[2] Daniel Yankelovich. "Changing Youth Values in the 70's." New York: JDR 3rd Fund, 1974.

[3] Gordon Cawelti. "The Effectiveness of Innovation." *Nation's Schools* 79 (4): 56-74; April 1967.

[4] William B. Fetters. *A Capsule Description of High School Seniors— Base Year Survey*. Washington, D.C.: Superintendent of Documents, U.S. Government Printing Office, 1974. p. 6.

In this booklet an effort has been made to: analyze the six reports; summarize and compare the recommendations, showing similarities as well as differences; evaluate the recommendations; and generate new ideas for secondary education, including research and curriculum.

2. Youth: Transition to Adulthood

The report, *Youth: Transition to Adulthood*,[1] was prepared by the Panel on Youth of the President's Science Advisory Committee. Need for the study grew out of the Committee's concern for strengthening the role played by the schools and other institutions in assisting youth's transition from adolescence to adulthood. Under the chairmanship of Professor James Coleman, the ten member panel met for a year to analyze the issue.

The panel members included a variety of scholars in such fields as history, sociology, economics, and education. Their report was published in June 1973. Presumably the recommendations of the study are under consideration by various governmental and educational institutions whose programs would be affected.

This provocative report, in the opinion of this reviewer, develops a much more thorough rationale for its recommendations than do other studies reviewed in this booklet. The Coleman report aims at experimentation in several ways for the express purpose of altering social policy as it affects the transition from youth to adulthood, particularly to the work world. It reflects the federal government's concern for the broad question of how our society and its institutions serve young people in their difficult transition to the world of work.

The Panel's Analyses

A central issue guiding the work of the panel members is stated early in the report:

[1] *Youth: Transition to Adulthood.* Report of the Panel on Youth of the President's Science Advisory Committee. Washington, D.C.: Superintendent of Documents, U.S. Government Printing Office, 1973. 190 pp.

Our basic premise is that the school system, as now constituted, offers an incomplete context for the accomplishment of many important facets of maturation.[2]

The panel observes that our society has passed through two phases in treating its youth. In the work phase, young people were put to work as quickly as possible and now, in the schooling phase, they are kept in school as long as possible and thus out of economic productivity.

The panel proposes changes in schooling and work patterns which will give persons in the 14-24 year old age bracket measured responsibility affecting other people. Demographic data are presented showing that in 1973, the ratio of population aged 14-24 was approximately 46 percent of the 25-64 year olds, or just over 43 million persons.

Age Segregation: Several changes in society brought on by industrialization are discussed. One of these is the age segregation which has become the dominant form of organization in schools. In contrast to the one room schoolhouse containing at least eight grades, children today stay with their own age group for most of their schooling. The panel members contend that there is considerable benefit to age integration within the school, and certainly they feel that young people need more extensive contact with adults.

In the industrial age, young people have had decreasing opportunities to learn a vocation from their parents. The panel members feel, therefore, that our institutions should be restructured to restore this earlier custom.

Legal Status and Rights of Youth: The panel's report affords an excellent review of the changing status of youth from early child labor laws to the 27th Amendment, which granted 18 year olds the right to vote. Although the rights of children have periodically been articulated by prestigious groups, only recently have these rights come to be widely recognized and respected. The demands for application of due process in schools, however, followed very closely behind the U.S. Supreme Court decisions of the sixties.

Although many school districts have not yet been challenged, it has clearly been established that protection under the Constitution and Bill of Rights does not stop at the schoolhouse door. In many

[2] *Ibid.*, p. 2.

schools this has had a major impact on how they are administered. Arbitrary standards invoked vaguely under an *in loco parentis* doctrine, applying to such areas as clothing, hair, newspapers, and nonparticipation in administrative and curriculum matters have fallen in many schools. Further, some persons have seriously raised questions about the constitutionality of compulsory attendance.

Economic Aspects of Youth: The considerable dependency of most young people on their families is noted, further emphasizing the long delay current schooling patterns present to youths. This means that, for many youths, much of schooling is simply an abstraction. Even those who do find part-time work usually have only limited opportunities to learn very much about a prospective vocation.

This panel reports its view that young people are responsive to shifting job opportunity patterns as they make their own career choices. It is an incentive for them to pursue a particular career when they are assured there will be a demand for them upon graduation from high school or college.

In the immediate future, it is projected that there will continue to be an increase in the number of college graduates while there is little assurance that a sufficient quantity of professional jobs for such graduates will exist. The federal government's recognition of this fact has been evident recently as officials raise questions about continued federal support of teacher training institutions that are producing an oversupply of teachers in many fields.

Changing Young People and Their Culture: The report analyzes the substantial differences in rates of maturation within age groups and between sexes, and the general trend downward (about four months per decade) in the age at which puberty begins. The impact of these differences is often not well recognized by teachers insofar as their expectations of youth are concerned.

The youth culture is examined in terms of three characteristics about which one can generalize. A distinction is made between "adolescents" and "youth" with the latter referring to a transition stage leading to adulthood and including the post high school age period.

One of the characteristics described is "inward lookingness" or that tendency to identify with and learn from peer groups to a much greater extent than in earlier times. There is a substantial youth market in such areas as clothes, entertainment, politics, and music. It is interesting to note the impact youth's tastes have had on older generations with regard to these trends.

A second element characterizing youth culture is described as the "psychic attachment" of youth to their peer group. The panel suggests that earlier patterns of "going steady" are being replaced by a pattern of closeness among a small group of friends and that the drug culture may have encouraged this. The communal group may have become the emerging pattern in which close psychic attachment is provided.

The third element described is a "press toward autonomy" and is exemplified by youth's respect for those who successfully challenge adults. The appeal of James Dean and other anti-heroes is based on this element. Other factors discussed include the impact of modern communications technology on society, the concern of the young for the underdog, and youth's interest in change.

All of these elements are accurate descriptions of youth although their distaste for Holden Caulfield's "phony" people is a significant omission. Coleman's 1960 study of youth culture in high school refers to this briefly, but one suspects that many of the values held by youths of that day are much different in the same age group now.

Summary of Recommendations

The following represents a summary and abstraction of the major recommendations which conclude the report. So that the reader can examine the report in its entirety, page numbers referring to the original report are inserted.

1. *Specialized High Schools and Free Choice (pp. 152-54):* In a reversal of Conant's famed support of the comprehensive high school in 1959, the panel believes youth will sometimes be better served by the clear mission of specialized high schools. These specializations might include such areas as science, performing arts, humanistic studies, industrial areas such as printing and publishing, and medical services. Obviously this has more application to urban areas or other multiple high school districts. The alternative school concept is a powerful idea well under way in many communities and

is difficult to oppose since it promotes diversity and yet retains traditional education for parents and students who desire it.

2. *School Size (pp. 154-56):* This recommendation implies that youth's needs might well be better met if high schools were permitted to be no larger than 500 students. Arguments advanced for smaller schools include reduced age segregation, less teacher specialization, and improved interpersonal relations between faculty and students. The possibilities for accomplishing this include the school-within-a-school organization or dual membership in large and small schools where necessary.

3. *Role Diversity for Youths in School (p. 156):* A particular emphasis here is for students to have the opportunity for tutoring younger pupils in the school thus affording a break from the age segregation that the report criticizes. A helping relationship to others encourages in youths a feeling that others are indeed dependent upon them. Tutoring has been extremely successful in many schools and most report that a tutor's conceptual understanding is improved in addition to that of the younger child being taught.

4. *The School as Agent for the Young (pp. 156-57):* This recommendation would have school personnel deploying students out to other community institutions for certain learning purposes. School functions should be reduced to more academic ones. Examples of this might include expansion of cooperative education or work-study programs and involvement of youth in public service activities. This is sometimes referred to as "action learning" and is now being widely advocated.

5. *Work-Study Programs (pp. 157-60):* The panel contends that even college-bound students would not suffer if they attend school for half days only. It is recommended that schools experiment with plans of half-day school and half-day work patterns and with plans in which students leave school and work full days for a period of time and then return to school.

6. *Work Organizations That Incorporate Youth (pp. 160-63):* This recommendation would induct youth into industries or agencies that would design learning roles for them. This would become a responsibility of business and agencies but they would need to receive public financial support with the following reasoning given:

For a firm to carry out public educational functions necessarily increases its costs and makes the firm noncompetitive in the market where its products or services are sold.[3]

Implicit in that statement is the panel's belief that schools are to bear the costs of training workers for industry. This social policy issue will be discussed later in the critique.

7. *Youth Communities and Organizations (pp. 163-66):* Recommendations in this area propose establishment of nonresidential institutions for youth that are largely self-governed and which focus on community service. School learning would be a secondary goal. Government support is encouraged for adult sponsored youth organizations whose activities are directed toward public service. It should again be emphasized that the panel envisioned them as social experiments and the report contains specific suggestions for evaluing trial efforts.

8. *Removing Barriers to Youth Employment Opportunities (pp. 166-68):* The essence of these proposals would be to review at the federal and state levels occupational restrictions and legal constraints which currently complicate the transition from youth to the adult work world. Child labor laws, compulsory attendance laws, and other administrative procedures should be changed to facilitate the transition. A dual minimum wage, one lower for youths than for adult workers, is proposed as another experiment.

9. *Vouchers (pp. 169-71):* The voucher plan is recommended as a way to encourage youth to make their own educational decisions on schooling or skill acquisition. Such a plan would permit more of an "in and out" system than we now have and would, perhaps, better equalize governmental support than the present system which discriminates in favor of those attending college.

10. *Public Service Opportunities (pp. 171-73):* The panel recommends expansion of federally funded public service projects such as the Peace Corps, VISTA, Job Corps, and Teacher Corps. These programs currently reach a very insignificant number of young persons in the 14-24 year old age bracket. The panel recommends that this expansion should start in areas in which the young people would be in minimum conflict with the adult community.

[3] *Ibid.,* p. 161.

3. Continuity and Discontinuity

Most of the 20 reports produced by the Carnegie Commission on Higher Education, under the chairmanship of Clark Kerr, have dealt primarily with higher education. However, *Continuity and Discontinuity*,[1] published in August 1973, contains many recommendations relating to high schools. Incidentally, none of the 17 members of the Commission were practitioners in public or private precollegiate education. Of 14 persons reported as advisers to the Commission, one was a principal and one was an associate superintendent in public education.

Details as to how the Commission proceeded were not included in the part of the report dealing with the schools but considerable attention was given to research studies by individuals such as Coleman or by organizations such as the American Council on Education or the American College Testing Program.

This report reflects a foundation's concern for certain of the problems of the high schools. Actually there are implications in the report for schools and colleges, boards of education, state departments of education, and testing agencies.

The Commission's Analyses

The Commission's report traces four major phases in a hundred year history of school-college relations, with 1940-1970 as the third phase with 48 percent of college age youth enrolled in higher education by 1970. Much of the central concern of the report is directed

---

[1] Carnegie Commission on Higher Education. *Continuity and Discontinuity, Higher Education and the Schools*. New York: McGraw-Hill Book Company, August 1973. 116 pp. Reprinted with permission. Copyright © 1973 by the Carnegie Foundation for the Advancement of Teaching.

to Phase IV (1970-2000), by which time, it is hoped, there will be universal access to higher education.

Such a goal will be helped by the open admissions policies of community colleges, new kinds of institutions, and expanded forms of financial aid. The traditions of selectivity and competition for better students are criticized.

The quality of an institution should be determined by what it does for the students it enrolls, not by the characteristics of its entering students or by the record of its graduates. Simple input or output measures are not sufficient. The test of institutional quality should be the value added by the college experience itself.[2]

Problems of restrictiveness and arbitrary admissions requirements, encouraged by the now widely criticized Carnegie unit, are reviewed. The limitations in universal access to higher education will continue unless higher education alters many of its traditions. Special mention is made of the need for schools to continue and improve basic skills programs, especially reading and math.

The serious problem of multiple applications for college entrance is discussed along with some of the criticism of excessive reliance on test scores for admission. The panel members point out that without grades, class rankings, or test scores it is not possible to predict how well students will do in a particular institution. Their language, almost begrudging on this point, suggests their hearts really were not in the "value added" concept of institutional purpose.

The Commission's review of the general status of secondary education finds that although achievement levels vary greatly, mass education in the United States, judged by conventional standards, does reasonably well. Members of the Commission, like other researchers or analysts, suggest that an important contribution to the knowledge high school graduates have comes from contact with family, and from the press and other media.

Evidence is presented verifying that much of what is taught in the first two years of college has already been taught at the secondary level. Professional associations and local, state, and national organizations are encouraged to work on eliminating such overlaps and duplications.

[2] *Ibid.,* p. 39.

The failure of urban school systems is described as the "most pressing" of educational problems. The report finds this is especially true in terms of the basic skills and vocational education. Although diversity in the types of schools to be made available is encouraged, the comprehensive high school seems to have the Commission's support.

A very brief discussion is provided on the content of the general education component of comprehensive high schools. Although basic skills are again emphasized, new topics suggested for general education include economics, computer science, philosophy, psychology, and art. This is a very minor and weak part of the report.

The interdependence of schools and colleges in the production of textbooks and instructional materials is noted. The costs associated with publication of new materials tend to limit experimentation in this area and, in general, the relationship among teachers, publishers, local curriculum committees, and university scholars is vague and uncertain. At best this relationship does not lend itself to systematic and continuous updating of materials.

Some newer educational practices are reviewed, particularly those encouraging alternative ways of obtaining an education or a diploma. A plan for a regional consortium of schools and colleges in New York State is described here which proposes to provide counseling services and learning options aimed at the External High School Diploma.[3] The plan would aim to use community resources much more widely and to devise ways of giving credit for such experiences.

The panel believes new structures in American education might help prevent some of the current discontinuity and might further encourage universal access to higher education. The idea of "middle colleges" is proposed which would be institutions providing for grades 11 through 14.

Various grade consolidation opportunities are suggested, such as the 3 year bachelor's degree program and the reduction of the 13 year K-12 sequence of learning down to 12 years. The need for enabling students to more easily "test out of" graduation requirements (a procedure already adopted in Oregon) is mentioned along

---

[3] For a more complete discussion of this plan see: Stephen K. Bailey, Francis U. Macy, and Dom F. Vichers. *Alternative Paths to the High School Diploma.* Reston, Virginia: National Association of Secondary School Principals, 1973. 63 pp.

with a plan for advancing college credits to high school seniors. Accrediting agencies are encouraged to promulgate such an idea.

Few new ideas appear in the section on training teachers and administrators. The idea of teacher centers as a more viable means of in-service education is encouraged and closer cooperation between higher education and the elementary and secondary schools is repeatedly stated as being essential to strong programs. Greater collaboration between schools and colleges is a recurring emphasis throughout the report.

Summary of Recommendations

The following list includes all of the recommendations in the Commission's report [4] with page numbers from the original study cited for reference. The reader is encouraged to study the entire report for a better grasp of the rationale underlying each recommendation.

Recommendation 1: Both public and private institutions should give careful attention to admissions policies suitable to an era characterized by universal access to the total system of higher education and by a no-growth enrollment trend. Public agencies, including coordinating councils and state planning commissions, should determine general policies on student admissions within state systems, including policies with respect to number of places, equality of access by race, age, and sex, and the level of academic admissibility among types of institutions. Decisions on individual students should be left to each campus (p. 39).

Recommendation 2: Colleges should develop admissions programs to seek out new constituencies, including high school juniors as well as adults and transfers from two-year colleges (p. 40).

Recommendation 3: To help maintain differentiation of function and to reduce excessive tension within state systems, two steps should be taken: (a) There should be experimentation on a large scale with doctor of arts degrees as a teaching alternative to the research Ph.D.; and (b) There should be a redefinition of institutional quality to focus upon the value added by the college experience itself (p. 40).

Recommendation 4: Colleges and testing agencies should work together in developing appropriate criteria and measures of value added to reflect a diversity of institutional objectives and outcomes (p. 40).

[4] Carnegie Commission on Higher Education, *op. cit.*, pp. 39-108.

Recommendation 5: Colleges should review their admissions requirements and, except for competence in the basic skills of reading, writing, and arithmetic, should not require or suggest particular courses of study at the secondary level unless such requirements or suggestions are tied explicitly to the colleges' own degree requirements, or to those of the system of which they are a part (p. 43).

Recommendation 6: High school students should be encouraged to study mathematics sequentially throughout secondary school in order to keep options open to college programs, jobs, and careers requiring background in mathematics (p. 43).

Recommendation 7: Colleges should closely examine their admissions policies with respect to sex, race, and age. They should then be certain that their admissions practices implement those policies that relate to social justice in higher education. Separate prediction equations for men and women, minority students, and adults should be developed and, where feasible, differential prediction by general field of study should be used (p. 46).

Recommendation 8: Testing agencies should initiate the development of a family of admissions and placement tests, with special versions prepared for individuals with particular educational and career aspirations (p. 46).

Recommendation 9: Schools, colleges, and testing agencies should work together in developing a complete and coherent information system that enables sound decision making by both students and colleges. Colleges should prepare frank, accurate, and complete descriptive materials, so that students will know as much about colleges as the colleges know about students (p. 49).

Recommendation 10: Students in elementary and high school should be counseled through a variety of resources—counselors, written materials, community-based people, as well as college students (minority students and women, in particular) (p. 49).

Recommendation 11: College admissions officers should be appointed with great care because their work is intimately tied to the primary mission of the institution. If possible, they should have both faculty status and a prominent place in the administrative hierarchy (p. 49).

Recommendation 12: In those areas where multiple college applications are a problem, clearinghouse operations utilizing single application forms, transcripts, and school report forms should be developed. Concern for the small amount of college autonomy involved should be less important than better service to students (p. 52).

Recommendation 13: Experimentation with college admission practices should be encouraged. In particular, more experimentation is needed to determine the quality of testing as a basis for admission and placement, the importance of student motivation and life experience as indicators of promise, and the feasibility of deferred admissions as a means of providing educational flexibility for students (p. 52).

Recommendation 14: Local school boards, with community and professional assistance, should identify the overall ends and objectives of the public schools, deliberately encourage experimentation with a diversity of means to those objectives, and insist upon accountability from teachers and administrators (p. 64).

Recommendation 15: Improvement of the nation's schools is the first educational priority in the nation; and within the schools improvement in the basic skills, especially in large city schools, is the first priority. Colleges and universities should recognize this fact and help to provide the resources, incentives, and rewards for faculty members who commit themselves to this task (p. 67).

Recommendation 16: Each state should undertake a review and analysis of the general education requirements for graduation from high school. Objectives should be clearly established and new means to these objectives should be explored, including the possibility that students can "test out of" graduation requirements. In addition, the relationship of general education at the high school to that at the college level, especially in grades 13 and 14, should be explored with a view toward ways that the general education requirements at both levels might be linked together to provide continuity and to prevent wasteful overlap and duplication. School and college faculty members should work together on this set of problems under the sponsorship of local, state, and national organizations such as the College Board and professional associations. More of the responsibility for general education should be assumed by the high schools (pp. 69-70).

Recommendation 17: Each state through its coordinating mechanisms should study carefully and define the roles of public high schools, area vocational schools, community colleges, and proprietary schools with respect to vocational and technical programs (p. 71).

Recommendation 18: Curriculum development in the humanities and social studies has lagged behind mathematics and science. Schools and colleges, together with funding agencies, should foster new programs and approaches (p. 73).

Recommendation 19: The Carnegie Commission recommends a

major national study of the entire set of relationships that exists between school systems, state bureaucracies, school and college teachers, and the educational materials industry in the production and selection of materials. The purpose of the study would be to seek ways to improve the system by which curricular materials are chosen, created, and marketed. Such a study should shed light as well upon the difficulties and problems associated with the widespread adoption of educational technology (p. 74).

Recommendation 20: Schools and colleges alike should remember that experimentation carries with it the price of accountability. No new programs at either level should be initiated without clear criteria for evaluation (p. 77).

Recommendation 21: Schools and colleges should experiment with different structural models designed to provide a student with options that will enable him to find the right program at the right time. Such experimentation challenges the current structure and its traditional break between school and college at the end of grade 12. Liberal arts colleges should consider enrolling students as early as grade 11 and awarding the bachelor's degree after grade 14 or 15; there should be experimentation with public education at age four; some school systems should eliminate a year from the K through 12 sequence; other school systems should stress general education equivalent to that found at good colleges; students should be able to "test out of" high school graduation requirements; there should be expanded programs of college credit for the senior year of high school, concurrent enrollment of students in school and college, and early admission to college; options other than college attendance should be made available for high school graduates (p. 83).

Recommendation 22: At present too many white, middle-class teachers are prepared in essentially nonspecific ways for general purpose assignments. The problems of the large urban schools, small rural schools, bilingual-bicultural schools, and wealthy suburban school districts require teachers trained for these separate constituencies. University faculties of arts and sciences and education should concentrate more upon training teachers for different kinds of schools. Because of the variety of tasks there can be no single model of a teacher-training program, and the National Council for the Accreditation of Teacher Education and state accrediting associations should encourage diversity. A common element in all preservice programs should be an emphasis upon bringing theory and practice together in clinical settings (p. 96).

Recommendation 23: Greater emphasis should be placed on in-service education of a different kind from that traditionally available.

Local teacher centers that focus on teachers' problems and that utilize the resources of the university should be encouraged and their effects carefully evaluated (p. 96).

Recommendation 24: Special efforts should be made to recruit able administrators from outside the field as well as members of minority groups and women into the profession of school administration (p. 99).

Recommendation 25: Given the diversity of school districts, there can be no single model of an administrator training program. Common elements in all programs should be the use of the resources of the whole university and experimentation with different ways of combining theory and practice in clinical settings (p. 100).

Recommendation 26: Greater emphasis should be placed on in-service training as a way of keeping administrators up-to-date and as a vehicle for school improvement (p. 100).

Recommendation 27: Universities, in conjunction with state school boards associations, should experiment with various means of providing school board members with information on crucial issues (p. 100).

Recommendation 28: Colleges and universities should encourage school-college collaboration on substantive matters through promotion and reward policies that recognize the importance of such activities (p. 103).

Recommendation 29: Though often different in temperament, training, and style, school and college teachers and administrators must work together to reduce many of the present undesirable discontinuities in the relationships between school and college (p. 108).

Recommendation 30: Activities having to do with the substantive matters discussed in this report should be initiated by five different agencies: state education offices, educational institutions, testing agencies, foundations, and the federal government (p. 108).

4. The Reform of Secondary Education

The National Commission on the Reform of Secondary Education was established in 1972 by the Charles F. Kettering Foundation. The Commission was charged with making a thorough study of secondary education and preparing recommendations on how these schools can better serve that age group. The 20 member Commission was chaired by B. Frank Brown of /I/D/E/A/, a Kettering affiliate. The members came from several different professional associations of educators, the PTA, the school board association, higher education, and also included three students and one teacher.

The Commission established panels of teachers, parents, students, and administrators involving about 800 participants representing every state. These panels were surveyed on various questions throughout the year-long work of the Commission. The Commission members met periodically and had a variety of resource people stimulate their thinking about the needs of high schools.

This report [1] was well conceived in terms of its involvement of persons affected and the representativeness of the Commission. The results of the various panels' attitudes toward the recommendations were included in the appendix to the report.

The Commission's Analyses and Rationale

The introductory pages of the report point out the effect of a declining birthrate on school enrollment and predicts that by 1984 no new high schools will be needed except replacements. This will

[1] National Commission on the Reform of Secondary Education. *The Reform of Secondary Education: A Report to the Public and the Profession.* New York: McGraw-Hill Book Company, 1973. 188 pp. Reprinted with permission.

19

result in the demand for far fewer teachers and will leave an older teacher force to face a youth population with increasingly difficult needs.

This period of shrinking enrollment is seen as a time for high schools to improve their instructional programs and for developing alternative paths to graduation. The Commission characterizes 1962-1972 as a "decade of innovation" which "had little or no lasting effect on the content of school programs or the quality of teaching and learning." [2]

Urban schools are described as on the verge of collapse in terms of declining achievement and attendance and with a rising incidence of crime.

A task force is following up on the Commission's recommendations during the current year (1973-74).

Summary of Recommendations[3]

Recommendation 1: Defining Secondary School Expectations. Every secondary school and its subordinate departments must formulate a statement of goals and develop performance criteria for students. Goals and objectives should be published in information bulletins for students and parents and be posted in a conspicuous place within the school building.

Recommendation 2: Community Participation in Determining Secondary School Expectations. Schools will not be able to achieve their purposes without increased help from the people in the communities they serve. Communities must participate in the formulation of goals and in continuing efforts to refine and adapt the statements of goals and objectives. The communities as a whole, not solely the subsection called schools, must achieve the goals.

Recommendation 3: The Basis for Curricular Revision. The high schools should no longer be required to perform purely custodial functions. Attempts to keep in school adolescents who do not wish to be there damage the environment for learning. The content of traditional high school curricula should be revised to eliminate busy-work components designed merely to occupy the time of adolescents who are in school only because the law requires it. Revitalization of the curriculum will require attention to the earlier maturation of adolescents. Intelligent evaluation

---

[2] *Ibid.*, p. 8.
[3] *Ibid.*, pp. 13-22.

of curricular revision must grow from valid measurements of the degree to which students are achieving the stated goals and objectives of their school.

Recommendation 4: Teacher Training. Teacher training institutions should revise their programs so that prospective teachers are exposed to the variety of teaching and learning options in secondary education. New teachers should be able to work in several instructional modes.

Extensive in-service programs should be instituted to retrain teachers presently employed to equip them with a greater variety of approaches and skills. This need will become increasingly acute as the decline in birthrate encumbers the schools with aging teaching staffs.

Recommendation 5: Bias in Textbooks. State legislatures must ensure that procedures are established so that textbooks and materials used in the schools do not present inaccurate accounts of the contributions of various ethnic groups or inaccurate portrayals of the role of women.

Recommendation 6: Bias in Counseling. Counselors should ensure that all students, regardless of sex or ethnic background, are afforded equal latitude and equally positive guidance in making educational choices.

Recommendation 7: Affirmative Action. Every high school should establish an affirmative action committee composed of students, former students, faculty, and community representatives. The purpose of this committee is to examine and report to the administration on instances of inequality and discrimination involving students or groups of students at the school.

Recommendation 8: Expanding Career Opportunities. Secondary schools must realign their curricula to provide students with a range of experiences and activities broad enough to permit them to take full advantage of career opportunities in their communities. To meet this objective, basic components of the school program will have to be offered in the late afternoon or in the evening for some students.

Recommendation 9: Career Education. Career education advisory councils including representatives of labor, business, community, students, and former students should be established to assist in planning and implementing career education programs in comprehensive high schools.

Career awareness programs should be initiated as an integral part of the curriculum to assure an appreciation of the dignity of work.

Opportunities for exploration in a variety of career clusters should be available to students in grades 8 through 10.

In grades 11 and 12, students should have opportunities to acquire hard skills in a career area of their choice. This training should involve experience in the world outside school and should equip the student with job-entry skills.

Recommendation 10: Job Placement. Suitable job placement must be an integral part of the career education program for students planning to enter the labor force upon leaving school. Secondary schools should establish an employment office staffed by career counselors and clerical assistants. The office should work in close cooperation with the state employment services. Agencies certifying counselors for secondary schools should require such counselors to show experience in job placement as a condition for granting initial certification.

Recommendation 11: Global Education. The education of the nation's adolescents must be superior to that of their parents. Part of this superiority must be an enhanced sense of the globe as the human environment, and instruction to this end must reflect not only the ancient characteristics of the world, but emerging knowledge of biological and social unity. All secondary school students should receive a basic global education.

New instructional material for global education must be prepared if this recommendation is to be effective. State departments of education should require teacher training institutions to design programs which prepare teachers to present such programs.

Recommendation 12: Alternative Paths to High School Completion. A wide variety of paths leading to completion of requirements for graduation from high school should be made available to all students. Individual students must be encouraged to assume major responsibility for the determination of their educational goals, the development of the learning activities needed to achieve those goals, and the appraisal of their progress.

Recommendation 13: Local Board Responsibilities for Funding Alternatives. Whenever a student chooses an acceptable alternative to the comprehensive high school, local school boards should fund his education at the level of current expenditure computed for other students.

Recommendation 14: Credit for Experience. Secondary schools should establish extensive programs to award academic credit for accomplishment outside the building, and for learning that occurs on-the-job, whether the job be undertaken for pay, for love, or for its own sake. Community involvement will, of course, be required in such a program and should be as encompassing as possible.

Recommendation 15: Secondary Level Examination Program. The College Level Examination Board should expand its College Level Examination Program to include a comparable Secondary Level Examination Program. The tests should be routinely administered quarterly or monthly to help adolescents to obtain credit for work done outside the classroom.

Recommendation 16: Broadcast Television. Major funding sources, including both foundations and the National Institute of Education, should initiate and support extensive research into the influence of television on students' attitudes, perceptions, and life styles. The purpose of this research should be to suggest changes in school curricula and instructional approach.

The broadcasting industry should establish media fellowships designed to afford secondary school teachers and instructional leaders the opportunity to study the use of broadcast commercial television for educational purposes.

Recommendation 17: Classroom Use of Broadcast Material. Copyright laws and union contracts should be written to make sure that classroom use of broadcast materials copied off the air is not unnecessarily restricted. Television programs should never be asked to carry instructional burdens alone. Books and pamphlets must be specially and carefully prepared to accompany all instruction via television. Both the instructional television program and the printed materials should be available in public libraries as well as in schools.

Recommendation 18: Cable Television. When cable franchises are awarded, the local school system should have exclusive use of three channels during the daytime, with possible use of more as needed. At least one—and preferably all three—of these cable channels should continue to be available for nighttime viewing by school students or for purposes of adult education.

Recommendation 19: Flexibility of Alternative Programs. Differing time sequences—hourly, daily, weekly, yearly—must be made available so that educational programs can be adapted to the needs of individual students.

Schools are already moving away from the Carnegie Unit and are beginning to grant credit on the basis of competence, demonstrated experience, and a host of other assessments. It is recommended that this practice be expanded and that the Carnegie Unit become merely one of the alternative ways of granting credit.

Recommendation 20: Rank in Class. Articulation between secondary schools and post-secondary schools must be improved, with each level seeking to support the educational efforts of the other. Personnel representing both levels must cooperatively develop alternatives to grade-point average and rank in class for assessing the scope and quality of the education received by students at the secondary level. High schools should stop calculating student rank in class for any purpose.

Recommendation 21: Planning for School Security. All secondary school systems should develop security plans to safeguard students, faculty, equipment, and facilities. Specific procedures must be developed for faculty members to follow in case of disruption.

Recommendation 22: Records of Violence. State legislation should be enacted to require principals to file a detailed report on all serious assaults within schools. The information contained should form a data base from which security personnel could identify potential trouble areas and move to alleviate future problems.

Recommendation 23: Code of Student Rights and Obligations. Every secondary school should develop and adopt a code of student rights and obligations. This code should be published and distributed to every student. It should include all school rules, regulations, and procedures for suspension and expulsion with explanations of how students can defend themselves through established process.

Recommendation 24: School Newspapers. A school newspaper is a house organ which is operated, financed, and therefore controlled by the school system, which may be legally liable for its contents. In cases where students and school administrators become deadlocked over censorship, a student-faculty-community committee should decide the issue. Some schools may find it necessary to withdraw financial support, allowing students complete freedom of expression in what would then be entirely their own publication, with a corresponding liability for what is printed.

Recommendation 25: Right of Privacy. A student's school records must contain only factual information necessary to the educative process. The entire file must be available at all times for review by students and their parents but must not be accessible to "persons not in interest." Records should be forwarded to another school system, university, or prospective employer only at the written request of the student, his parents, or the receiving school.

That part of a student's records which pertain to his mental health should contain only entries made under the direction of the student's physician and must be kept separately from his academic records. The complete record or any of its contents should be released only to the student, his parents, or to his physician at the student's or parent's request.

Recommendation 26: Corporal Punishment. Several states have out-lawed corporal punishment with no resulting loss in control or authority. Corporal punishment should be abolished by statute in all states. In the modern world, corporal punishment is necessarily "cruel and unusual."

Recommendation 27: Student Activities. Scholarship should not be a requisite for participation in sports, band, singing, cheerleading, or other student activities important to the social development of adolescents. Neither the local school nor state activities associations should establish scholarship standards. Any student in good standing in a school should have the right to participate in any of the school's activities with the exception of honor societies specifically established to reward scholarship.

Recommendation 28: Compulsory Attendance. If the high school is not to be a custodial institution, the state must not force adolescents to attend. Earlier maturity—physical, sexual, and intellectual—requires an option of earlier departure from the restraints of formal schooling.

The formal school-leaving age should be dropped to age fourteen. Other programs should accommodate those who wish to leave school, and employment laws should be rewritten to assure on-the-job training in full-time service and work.

Recommendation 29: Free K-14 Public Education. The Congress of the United States in conjunction with state legislatures should enact legislation that will entitle each citizen to 14 years of tuition-free education beyond kindergarten, only 8 of which would be compulsory. The remaining 6 years should be available for use by anyone at any stage of his life. Congressional involvement is essential to assure equal access in an age of interstate mobility.

Recommendation 30: Youth Organizations. The National Association of Secondary School Principals, a professional organization for school administrators, currently operates two of the largest organizations affecting public high school youth: the National Student Council Association and the National Honor Society. The principals' group should dissociate itself from these organizations and help them become independent national youth organizations.

Recommendation 31: Sexism. School administrators and school boards, at both the state and local levels, must set forth commitments to eliminate all vestiges of sexism in the schools.

Areas of immediate concern are equal employment and treatment of the sexes in instructional and administrative positions, equal opportunities for female students to participate in all curricular areas, including career education, and the elimination of all courses required of only one sex.

Individual teachers should make sure they are not focusing their teaching toward either sex.

All female students who become pregnant should be permitted to remain in school for the full term of pregnancy if they wish to do so and their physician considers it feasible. They should be permitted to return to school following childbirth as soon as released by their physician. There must be no denial of the right to participate in activities because of pregnancy or motherhood, whether the girl is wed or unwed.

Recommendation 32: Females in Competitive Team Sports. School boards and administrators at the local level must provide opportunities for female students to participate in programs of competitive team sports that are comparable to the opportunities for males. The programs must be adequately funded through regular school budgets.

Outstanding female athletes must not be excluded from competition as members of male teams in noncontact sports. The fact that a school offers the same team sport for girls should not foreclose this option.

State activities associations should be required by statute to eliminate from their constitutions and bylaws all constraints to full participation in competitive team sports by females.

If state activities associations are to continue to have jurisdiction over female sports, they should be required by state statute to have equal sex representation on all boards supervising boys' and girls' athletics.

Compulsory Attendance

The most controversial of the recommendations is 28, dealing with compulsory attendance. The idea behind this recommendation is deceptively simple and will have appeal for some. There are many students who do not like school and who distract other students from their work. If schools, the reasoning goes, were freed from educating such students, but were expected to provide the schooling later when student motivation may be higher, the institution could do a better job with those remaining.

That logic and that policy are not going to compel schools to improve their instructional deficiencies. High school programs will be even more likely to lack vitality. The prospect of significant numbers of students ever coming back is highly questionable. Adults are involved in continuing education in large numbers because they have recognized a need at a particular time in their lives. But what if that need never is perceived?

Fundamentally, however, the recommendation to lower compulsory attendance laws to 14 years should be resisted because this would foster an elitism our society does not need. Many middle and upper class families place considerably more pressure on their young to stay in school than do lower class families. The former are better able to afford keeping their children in school. Until the Rodriguez decision is altered, low income families will continue to be denied the benefits of an equitable school finance system. Legislatures enacting this recommendation would only be furthering such inequities. It is doubtful if any of them will do this.

It is clear that public school education is weak in many respects. Moreover the urban areas have the most acute problems with limited resources for dealing with them. When attendance rates are 50 percent or below, boldly different and better alternatives must be made available to children of recent immigrants or from disadvantaged homes. Yet to give up on them is contrary to American optimism for its youth. When schools continue to fail after applying all that is known about motivation, human growth and development, and learning, then perhaps schools should let those go who cannot succeed at public education. This is a more fertile area for educators' efforts than simply waiting until student motivation is high.

The Commission's recommendations encouraging more alternative environments are well formulated. They argue for a more humane climate in schools and increased emphasis on self-direction for those who can handle it. More interaction between the school and the community can and should be accomplished under the direction of skilled teachers who have firsthand knowledge of the work world.

Prompt and courageous action should certainly be taken in those schools where security plans are failing to provide students the safety assurances needed. The unsafe conditions reported in some high schools are true and simply cannot be tolerated. Accurate records of assaults must be maintained and the entire faculty must work in cooperation with security personnel.

Goals

The Commission analyzed goals obtained from 37 states and used George Gallup to submit them to the various panels of people previously described. Respondees were asked to "substantiate the relevance of the goals" by rating the desirability of each of 13 goals and rating how well recent graduates reflect attainment of these goals. Findings were related to previously articulated national goals such as the Cardinal Principles of Secondary Education (1918), Educational Policies Commission (1938), and Goals for Americans (1960).

Schools taking these findings seriously would develop new programs or revise existing timid efforts in the direction of (a) career education, (b) economic understanding, (c) cultural pluralism, (d) clarification of values, (e) environmental studies, and (f) the humanities. Most of the other goals the Commission has formulated such as basic skills and citizenship are common to previous national goals.

All of these changes are desirable and reflect emerging curriculum developments in responsive schools. The goals section is weakened by a failure to distinguish clearly between content and goal matters. Little help is given to the principal or curriculum makers in determining how the schools can teach more in an already crowded curriculum. The goals section carries *no* rationale for some of the statements other than the degree of concurrence of referent groups.

The goal study, in general, was a useful one in that it pulled together trends at the state level. It is significant to note that 37 states do have goal statements. If this is so, what is the purpose of needs assessment in the local community? That is, why should administrators spend countless hours involving their community in assessing needs if states already have specific goals in mind?

The Commission recommends that each secondary school develop its own goal statements and performance criteria with community involvement included in forming such goals. One can fault the report, however, for failure to make the point that students must be involved, on a parity basis, along with other people who are less affected by educational decisions.

In general, it will be helpful for principals to examine carefully the Commission's goal statements in relation to the objectives and existing educational practices in their own schools. Having done this, much will remain to be accomplished to determine what the priorities should be in a given community.

Content

Recommendations for revitalizing the content include curriculum revision toward performance-based instruction, eliminating bias in instructional materials, career education, and global education.

The idea of performance-based instruction is a viable one and most appropriate at this time for *training* kinds of goals, such as reading, handwriting, and composition. While there are indices of performance in the arts, for example, schools would do better to *start* with performance-based instructional patterns in basic skill areas. (The report reiterates the findings of Project Talent which showed that writing ability of high school students is often inadequate. Competency levels should be established and greater emphasis should be given to this area.)

The importance of eliminating racism, sexism, and other kinds of instructional bias (against labor unions or big business, for example) should not be underestimated. State departments of education, professional organizations, school systems, and teachers should actively seek to assure that instructional materials do not continue to reinforce stereotypes or incorrect information.

The career education recommendation reflects a movement that has made much headway. More work-study programs are advocated. Principals responsible for promulgating this concept must understand that career education is to be viewed as a pervasive influence. Every teacher is expected to relate the occupational significance of material covered. All grade levels are to be involved. Every student would leave high school with a skill. Job placement services would be provided by the school.

Much has been written about the career education movement. Schools should examine their financial responsibility for career education and that of private industry before too great a proportion of scarce resources is allocated. Is it national policy that schools prepare workers for the private sector? If such preparation is a shared responsibility, who pays how much? This question of policy cannot be ignored or left vague.

The recommendation on global education is a needed emphasis in the schools. "Interglobal dependency" is, I believe, a more descriptive concept, but whatever it is called, it seems imperative to focus on resource scarcity, environmental education, and international politics and economics. It is interesting to note that although global education is a major recommendation in the content area, no mention is made of it in the goals section of the report.

Student Rights and Obligations

The recommendations dealing with student rights are valid. There should be a code of student rights and obligations in each school that provides for due process. Corporal punishment should be outlawed. There should not be absolute prerequisites for participation in student activities, and student records should be available for examination by students or parents and sent out to others only at their request.

Student Organizations

The recommendations that NASSP no longer be responsible for operating the National Student Council Association and National Honor Society deserve careful study by the governing bodies involved. There is some doubt the association or society would survive without NASSP support. Both probably need more vitality and leadership in their activities. A much more basic question is the role of student councils. If the National Student Council Association helps local councils become involved in an authentic and appropriate governance role, the relationship should be preserved. If the relationship does not help do this, NASSP should follow the recommendation of the Commission.

In summary, this report adds to a number of documents and individuals advocating more "action learning" and alternative routes to graduation. These are credible ideas that should make the secondary school years more productive for many students. It has become clear that sources outside the school are often more powerful than is conventional instruction. It will be useful to see if the performance-based idea, if adopted, will demonstrate that these experiences produce achievement that the schools will accept for credit. Despite my personal dissent on the compulsory attendance issue, this report is commended to readers for careful scrutiny and action.

5. American Youth in the Mid-Seventies

American Youth in the Mid-Seventies [1] grew out of a conference on this topic held in Washington, D.C., November 30-December 1, 1972. Sponsored by NASSP's National Committee on Secondary Education, the conference was financially supported by the Stone Foundation, the U.S. Office of Education, the U.S. Office of Economic Opportunity, the White House, and ACTION.

Attended by some 125 educational leaders from schools, universities, and other agencies, the conference focused on "action learning." This term, broadly defined, refers to a kind of curriculum in which the school provides learning opportunities out in the community to reduce the isolation of youth from the "real world." Sometimes referred to as experiential learning, this idea is similar to other programs described or recommended elsewhere in this booklet. Action learning also reflects a growing recognition among educators that high school teachers and instructional programs are increasingly unable to reach many young people either intellectually or socially.

The report reflects many of the concerns of a large professional association of persons primarily interested in secondary education. Papers given at the conference were categorized according to (a) the need for action learning programs, (b) institutional views on the issue, (c) research and evaluation, and (d) reports on action learning programs.

Need for Action Learning

Sidney Marland, at that time the Assistant Secretary for Education in the U.S. Department of Health, Education, and Welfare,

[1] National Association of Secondary School Principals, National Committee on Secondary Education. *American Youth in the Mid-Seventies*. Reston, Virginia: the Association, 1972. 104 pp. Reprinted by permission of the National Association of Secondary School Principals, copyright 1972, Washington, D.C.

asserted his advocacy of career education, pointing out he was continuing to avoid a precise definition of this area in the formative stages. Calling career education ". . . a change of heart and a change of mind . . . ," Marland reaffirmed the applicability of action learning to career education at the high school level.

Dr. Marland reported that in early 1972, approximately 1,350,000 youths between the ages of sixteen and twenty were unemployed. The Office of Education and the National Institute of Education were reported to be deeply involved in developing and implementing action learning programs in career education.

Congressman William Steiger from Wisconsin expressed concern for a continued high dropout rate and the "failure" label given to such young people. He warned that schools should not go overboard in providing action learning in career education programs at the expense of general education and basic skill programs. He also said that care must be taken to provide the kinds of supervision young people need to assume action learning experiences that are educative, and that present workers should not be displaced.

| | Ages: 16-21 | Percentages of Total | | Percentage Shift Over 10 Years |
		1960	1970	
Out of School	White male	40.4	38.0	− 6
	Non-white male	52.9	44.1	−17
	Non-white female	58.1	49.7	−14
	White female	52.0	45.3	−13
Unemployed (as percent of labor force)	White male	9.9	12.0	+21
	Non-white male	15.3	24.9	+63
	Non-white female	17.3	31.7	+83
	White female	7.8	13.4	+72
Not in Labor Force	White male	42.1	38.4	− 9
	Non-white male	49.5	51.0	+ 3
	Non-white female	69.9	59.6	−15
	White female	61.8	50.6	−18
	Ages: 14-19			
Married	White male	3.1	2.8	−10
	Non-white male	4.3	1.6	−63
	Non-white female	12.1	8.7	−28
	White female	13.3	9.6	−28

Table 1. *Changing Status of Youth: 1960-1970*

Insightful data on *American Youth in the Mid-Seventies* were presented by Robert Havighurst, Richard Graham, and Donald Eberly. Their information, taken from U.S. Census data, is cited in Tables 1 and 2.[2]

	(Percentages)					
	Male			*Female*		
	Total	*White*	*Black*	*Total*	*White*	*Black*
High school dropout	20	18	35	19	18	34
High school graduate	26	24	40	38	37	48
College 1-3 years	30	32	14	24	25	10
College graduate	25	26	11	19	20	8

Table 2. *Highest Educational Level Reached by Young People: 1971*

The authors arrived at the following conclusions from the 1960-1970 census data studied:

1. The number of teenagers during that period increased by 30 percent but the employment rate increased by 50 percent.

2. Teenage marriage rates decreased substantively—down by 28 percent for females, down 10 percent for white males and 63 percent for non-white males.

3. The number of young persons staying in school has continued to increase with some 80 percent graduating from high school; 25 percent of the age group were graduating from college compared to 19 percent ten years ago.

4. The unemployment rate for eighteen to nineteen year olds is 14 percent, but is much higher (24 percent) for non-white males—compared with a national unemployment rate of about 5 percent at this writing.

5. An estimated 20-30 percent of fifteen to twenty year olds remain in school or college but do not find it very satisfying in terms of finding a useful place in society.

6. Although a decade ago about half of the young women in the United States were married by age twenty, in 1971 this rate had fallen to 40 percent.

[2] *Ibid.*, p. 13. Source of statistics: U.S. Bureau of the Census. Series P-20. No. 224. March 1972.

This report also provides useful data on the number of public and private social service employment opportunities. The authors recommend adding action learning programs to the traditional pattern of growing up in America.

Institutional Views

UNIONS—John Sessions, Assistant Director of Education for the AFL-CIO, expressed a concern that education in a factory may not be superior to that in a classroom—that not all experiences in the community and work place will automatically be valuable. He criticized the nature of the emphasis Sidney Marland had placed on career education, saying that job placement alone was not satisfactory evidence of a quality program. He said quite pointedly, in looking at the career education models, that unions would not support employer-managed programs with no union voice in the policies, nor would unions ". . . permit the erosion of the negotiated wages structure." [3] He indicated that this will be a difficult problem to overcome if action learning becomes a popular notion—along with the equally larger problem of competition for jobs.

ACCREDITING AGENCIES—John Stanavage, Executive Secretary of the Secondary Commission of the North Central Association, generally expressed support of the action learning idea as one alternative. He indicated that at least the NCA, as one regional accrediting agency, was making efforts to increase the flexibility of its standards to accommodate this nontraditional mode of education. The guidelines and principles articulated in the Stanavage paper are well done and would be useful for planning purposes.

In a working paper for his governing board to consider, Stanavage proposes to alter the approach for accrediting "nonstandard" schools or those heavily committed to action learning as their primary instructional mode. The acceptance and evaluation process would be rather more like the accrediting procedure NCA uses for colleges and universities which is judging schools on the basis of how well they meet their stated goals.

[3] *Ibid.*, p. 39.

STATE DEPARTMENT OF EDUCATION—Robert Sigmon, Director of the North Carolina Internship Office of the North Carolina State Board of Education, reported that most state education agencies have given student action learning projects a low priority. His office serves to arrange, manage, and advocate "service-learning" internships for college students. Sigmon discussed problems associated with defining worthwhile tasks for students and recruiting students and cooperating agencies. A form for rating such internships was presented. This form would be useful in evaluating relationships between the intern and agency. He indicated that his office's function is to bridge the gap between public agencies needing help and students desiring such experiences.

Research and Evaluation

Richard Graham, Director of Education Programs for ACTION, reported on his own survey of research which has been done on learning through experience. Among the findings [4] that he reported were the following:

1. The most common practice is for schools to grant academic credits on the basis of time spent in work experience or voluntary service—a typical example might be to equate one classroom hour with two or three hours on the job.

2. If the hours per week in action learning situations do not exceed 15, there is apparently no adverse effect on academic achievement.

3. There is little empirical evidence supporting the contention that the action learning program results in the sought-for affective growth of adolescents.

4. Young persons who have experienced repeated failure in schooling and work need to achieve success before a "tipping point" in their personality occurs that will result in greater self-confidence and optimism.

5. Menial tasks in action learning programs do little for middle class students and may actually have negative effects on the poor.

6. Work experience in jobs which are immediately available seem to increase the chances of getting and keeping such jobs, and students who have had work experience tend to earn higher wages and report greater job satisfaction.

[4] *Ibid.*, pp. 76-80.

7. As a general rule, 60 to 70 percent of the skills needed in a job are acquired on the job.

8. After being out of high school for five years, only one person in five plans to remain in the occupation he chose in school and the new career choices reported tend not to be toward closely related careers.

Ernst Stromsdorfer, Associate Professor of Economics at Indiana University, discussed problems of designing research on action learning programs. He indicated that it was important for school people to learn more about the optimum mix of time spent in (a) formal learning, (b) on-the-job learning, (c) labor market work, (d) non labor market work, and (e) leisure. He was particularly concerned about research problems imposed on the bias inherent when students are permitted to select whether or not they will enter action learning programs. He proposes random assignment of students to experimental and control groups as a means of eliminating such bias.

Action Learning Projects

The section of the report on action learning projects is very limited, and two of the three programs reported deal with higher education. A far better source for examples of action learning programs is *The Greening of the High School*.[5] This volume reports a three day conference cosponsored by EFL and /I/D/E/A/, two institutions supported by the Ford and Kettering foundations. It was attended by some 35 persons with reasonable balance among government, foundations, private and professional organizations, and public school practitioners. None of the participants could be identified as curriculum specialists from either the university or public school sectors.

At this conference, former Commissioner of Education Harold Howe articulated his proposed "Ten Commandments" which followed themes consistent with several of these national reports. The examples of action learning programs are highly readable and include references to sources of further information.

[5] Ruth Weinstock. *The Greening of the High School*. New York: Educational Facilities Laboratory, 1973. 88 pp. Also available upon order from /I/D/E/A/, P.O. Box 628, Dayton, Ohio 45419.

Among the various examples of action learning programs described were: [6] "Five O'Clock High" in Las Vegas; the Connecticut Citizen Action Group involving students in political activities to improve the environment; the Monroe High School in New York City which brings the outside world into the schoolhouse; the Human Resources Center in Pontiac, Michigan, which affords varied learning opportunities in a community-school setting.

The report discusses some of the space and faculty implications of a different kind of high school program. Obstacles to change are reviewed with suggestions made for accelerating the change process.

Oregon is one state that has pioneered in revising the high school program through new State Board of Education regulations [7] which specify "survival competencies" required for graduation.

[6] *Ibid.*, pp. 32-33.

[7] Dale Parnell. "Survival Competencies: New Oregon Graduation Requirements." *Educational Leadership* 31 (5): 390-92; February 1974.

6. National Panel on High Schools and Adolescent Education

In early 1972 Assistant Secretary for Education Sidney Marland instructed a panel of some 22 persons to analyze the strengths and weaknesses of the nation's high schools in terms of their service to individuals and society at large and to then make recommendations for improvement. The panel was chaired by John Henry Martin and included an interdisciplinary mix of scholars from economics, sociology, psychology, management, and human development. The panel included two students, four U.S. Office of Education staff members, and one practicing school superintendent. Some 24 background papers were delivered, and the panel also visited schools and interviewed educational leaders.

The summary used in this report was obtained from an unpublished manuscript [1] prepared for the panel but no information was obtained as to when full publication of the report is due. Because of the tentative and unpublished nature of this information regarding the panel's work, and because some of the papers are repetitious, only the major points of view that differ from those in the other reports are discussed here.

The Panel's Analyses

Following are some of the major observations in the papers:

1. There is a growing public awareness of the inability of the high school to serve its youth, and that typical "student control" measures cannot be applied.

[1] John Henry Martin. "Chairman's Digest." U.S. Department of Health, Education, and Welfare, Office of Education, Panel on High Schools and Adolescent Education. Mimeographed. April 1974.

2. It is emphasized that the high school retains the crucial functions of transmitting our culture and history, and providing preparation for adulthood and citizenship.

3. The present system of schooling isolates 14-17 year olds from younger children and adults, and from other institutions in the community.

4. Schools have tended to underestimate the significance of earlier maturation in the present generation and instead are expected to serve a babysitting function or, as the panel put it, we maintain high schools as "aging vats."

5. The basic purposes for which high schools exist are not well served by the present curriculum structure.

6. There is a greater need for comprehensive education than for preservation or extension of the comprehensive high school concept.

7. High schools have proven to be the most difficult institution to change fundamentally, yet, while many have very large enrollments, there has been only limited application of behavioral science knowledge about organizations to this level of schooling.

8. High schools have accepted responsibility for more tasks than they are capable of fulfilling, and thus they are marginal institutions with respect to many tasks assumed.

Summary of Recommendations

It will be useful to the reader to scrutinize carefully the papers prepared for this panel's report. Although this group's processes apparently are not as clearly conceived as those of the National Commission on the Reform of Secondary Education, its focus is somewhat broader in scope and develops a smaller number of issues perhaps more thoroughly. This group's efforts, as originally requested by Dr. Marland, are directed more toward the possible role the federal government might play in stimulating needed change in the education of adolescents.

These papers echo others in calling for extension of the high school out in the community in a broad sense. The contributions of other agencies should be identified and used. Programs calling for joint participation of adolescents and adults are urged. The arts, career education, and government are curricular areas thought to be particularly appropriate for such an approach. Authentic student involvement in government, not just token representation, is advocated. Schooling should be provided during hours other than the regular school day.

Opportunities for increased work experience could be provided through a Community Career Education Center. Barriers to student opportunities for work experience and volunteer service should be removed.

Alternative schools for meeting specialized student needs in such areas as journalism or the arts should be provided as a way to decentralize large schools and should be more responsive to the deep interests some adolescents have already acquired. Community based sites or satellite centers for learning are strongly emphasized.

Reduction of compulsory attendance at all-day sessions to a two-to-four hour day is recommended. If students demonstrate they cannot handle such freedom, the compulsory time would be increased, but high schools are urged to move away from their babysitting function.

Citizen and student participation are urged as schools undertake changes in their structure and program. Tryouts of new programs should be carried out in limited situations rather than completely converting a system before effects are known.

Considerable attention is given to the economics of present staffing patterns and new ways of scheduling and arranging students and teachers together are urged. The National Institute of Education and the U.S. Office of Education are called upon to support research on the change process. Although the need for such research is not well articulated in this manuscript, the panel touches on this critical area in discussing the problem of nonresponsive institutions and bureaucratic structures.

The panel recommends that a comprehensive education for adolescents includes experiences in what they call five "curricular domains." These are briefly described under the headings of (a) personal values, (b) citizenship, (c) the arts, (d) the humanities, and (e) technics or career education. Presumably the final report will develop these "domains" more thoroughly so they can be scrutinized. Even in this brief form, more attention is given to the substantive curriculum issues which are not well covered in the other reports and which will be discussed in the final chapter of this book.

Another significant idea is introduced dealing with increasing
". . . the power and consequences of education" rather than reducing
the compulsory attendance age requirements. All the other reports
make the assumption that action learning is the desirable, indeed
perhaps the only way to motivate many adolescents. The prac-
ticality of the action learning idea in large urban centers remains
to be seen. Sending thousands of 14-18 year olds out into the
community would create an enormous addition to the labor market.
The alternative, of course, is to make instruction more powerful
and vital. Hopefully there are a few believers around willing to
experiment in this direction.

7. A Curriculum Critique

The half-dozen national reports reviewed here reflect much concern for the adequacy and vitality of the high school. Such concern is voiced whether by the foundations, the federal government, or the professional association for secondary school principals. In many respects, the recommendations of these studies support programs that have actually been emerging in more responsive schools during the past few years. It is my hope, however, in spite of my own recognition of the urgency of the present need for vitalizing the high school program, that caution should and will be exercised in responding to many of the proposals that have been put forward in these reports.

One senses a sort of defeatism and an anti-intellectual stance in these reports. Some of the panelists appear to have made the assumption that adequate schooling is unlikely to be made available to most adolescents. Again, an increasing responsibility for career education is implied repeatedly with public education assuming the costs. School officials will, therefore, need to decide on these two issues and to guide implementation accordingly.

Alternative Paths to Graduation

Many of the recommendations seem to this writer to have merit and the most often recurring ideas are summarized in the listing that follows. Generally the reports encourage schools to broaden the paths that high school students would have as options for seeking the diploma.

1. *Action Learning*—Designing programs that are generally

located out in the community in public work or social service situations but that are not menial in nature; these experiences would be either paid or nonpaid.

2. *In-Out Patterns*—Providing encouragement for students to enter and to leave formal schooling for work, service, or travel without penalty or disfranchisement, presumably returning when better motivated; voucher plans would be used to facilitate this idea.

3. *Competency Testing-Early Admissions*—Developing programs which assure that students who can "test out of" a subject are given the opportunity to do so; and which encourage students who are ready to enter higher education institutions at earlier ages.

4. *Alternative Schools*—Larger school systems are urged to develop specialized (as contrasted with comprehensive) high schools in order to increase their pupil-retaining power. Other alternative schools might be organized within larger institutions, but might concentrate on particular areas such as the arts or a career field, or on fundamentally different school environments (for example, less regimented, or broader student participation in setting goals).

5. *Basic Skills Competencies*—Much encouragement is given to schools to increase their efforts in assuring that certain minimum competencies be required for graduation in such areas as mathematics, reading, and composition. Students would be expected to assume more responsibility to see that these competencies are reached.

6. *Career Education*—Several reports have recommendations for helping young people make a smoother transition to the work world. Action learning experiences in work-study programs and social service projects are recommended, along with new roles for agencies other than schools to perform.

7. *Community Education Centers*—The establishment of educational institutions away from the conventional setting are recommended to serve people of all ages, not just youth. These would be similar to community schools but would have broader functions for helping direct learners of all ages toward experiences from which they might benefit. Schools operating at other than regular school

hours are encouraged in this connection. This proposal would also aim at reducing age segregation, a concern also mentioned in the reports.

Although the recommendations themselves touch on a much larger variety of topics, advocacy of these alternative paths to graduation will come through strongest to persons who may be involved in interpreting what they mean for a school situation.

Criticisms of the Recommendations

Three of the panels or commissions did not have any high school principals or curriculum specialists among their membership. Of a total of 49 persons in the three groups, there were two practitioners. While a mix of persons from various disciplines is useful, a better representation of students, females, teachers, principals, and members of minority groups would likely have caused any of the panels to probe certain issues more deeply. In addition, the following criticisms can be made of the reports, with certain exceptions noted.

1. *School Climate*—Virtually no attention was given to the problem of school climate, some aspects of which are highly distracting or annoying to many students. Inadequate teacher-student personal relationships, petty rules, regimentation, and lack of a trusting relationship are realities for students in many schools. A humanistic climate in schools can be fostered and can do much to overcome other inadequacies of the secondary school setting.

2. *Futures Orientation*—Little significant discussion was provided to help principals or curriculum specialists to look ahead in curriculum planning. Apparently operating on a social utility basis of curriculum making, the recommendations focus more on today's need than on that of the years ahead. Little concern was expressed for the nature of the society that today's youth should be helping to create. No rationale appears for a recommendation calling for a two-to-four hour school day during an era in which knowledge is accumulating at an accelerating rate.

3. *Curriculum Content and Learning Strategies*—In recent years the high school has been asked to "add on" or to "integrate"

instruction dealing with social or personal concerns such as drugs, sex, leisure, environment, morality, death, highway fatalities, plus consumer education and ethnic studies. The Commission on the Reform of Secondary Education encourages "global education," and the Office of Education report might well amplify its brief descriptions of the curriculum fields it proposes.

Otherwise, the reports provide little help in shifting away from the traditional curriculum which has so long dominated the high school. No new sense of direction for the school's curriculum emerges from these reports except that learning should be more experiential. Therefore, it might be anticipated that the "patch-on" curriculum will continue since, most assuredly, an accelerated rate of social change will produce new demands to which the schools will be expected to respond. Nevertheless, one encouraging element is contained in these recommendations: the schools are asked to limit the number of goals or tasks for which they must accept responsibility.

4. *Change Mechanisms*—Only the Office of Education report gives much indication of how difficult it is for the high school as an institution to change. The recommendations calling for the federal government to provide help to middle management are overdue and are encouraging. Applications of behavioral science techniques to the school organization will be necessary if high schools are to become more responsive and relevant. If a system of renewal can be built into the curriculum, there is some hope that schools will be better able to hold their students and to serve their needs more effectively. As many larger school districts have decentralized, it has been typical for a whole new set of organizational problems to emerge. There must be built-in flexibility and vitality in these new programs if they are to provide the responsiveness that is being sought.

Present Curriculum Deficiencies

The dominant pattern of curriculum organization in high schools can best be described as subject-centered. Although in recent years there has been some change in the grade placement of subjects such as science, history, or mathematics, students still take *courses* which are pretty much limited to academic content drawing on one subject field. Teachers are trained and classes are scheduled for this kind of curriculum pattern.

Attempts to alter this pattern substantively have appeared through such descriptors as the core or common learnings curriculum. Team teaching for a time was thought to be a way of organizing schools to overcome the separate subjects curriculum. Advocates of such interdisciplinary approaches have generally not fared very well because of tradition and resistance to change since both the public and the academicians fear that the contribution of a particular "discipline" will thereby be diminished.

The case for a more interdisciplinary approach to the curriculum has been made elsewhere by several persons.[1] Some contend that the lack of vitality of the present high school curriculum is due to its failure to come to grips with many issues about which young people are highly concerned. Some examples are the following:

... On the issue of our deteriorating environment and resource scarcity, only a few schools have developed instructional programs which draw on the economic, political, and scientific aspects of the problem. Young people are thus ill equipped to come to grips with the many forces operating to minimize any real progress on the issue. Not much progress can ever be expected by teaching just the history or just the scientific aspects of pollution.

... In the arts, a few unified humanities courses are being taught but most students have only limited opportunities in this area except for those in performance groups. As a result, there is a distinct garishness about the architecture in many communities and cultural events struggle for survival even in metropolitan areas. Our tastes for motion pictures have been "leveled" to the point at which sex and violence seem to be the only topics that will draw wide audiences.

... Most students (Americans) have only the barest notion of the economics of private enterprise, inflation, recession, prices, or unemployment. Until there is broad public understanding as to which social group suffers when a given corrective policy is insti-

[1] See especially: Ronald J. Hyman, editor. *Approaches in Curriculum.* Englewood Cliffs, New Jersey: Prentice-Hall, Inc., 1973. 225 pp.

tuted, it can be anticipated that tedious debates over union and management roles in private enterprise will continue but nothing will be resolved based on comprehension of the values ultimately involved.

The typical curricular experience, then, might be depicted as shown in Figure 1. It is a subject-centered, traditional curriculum in which the subjects serve not as means, but as ends in themselves. Students tend to know more about Monroe's early nineteenth century presidency than they do about the nature of U.S. involvement

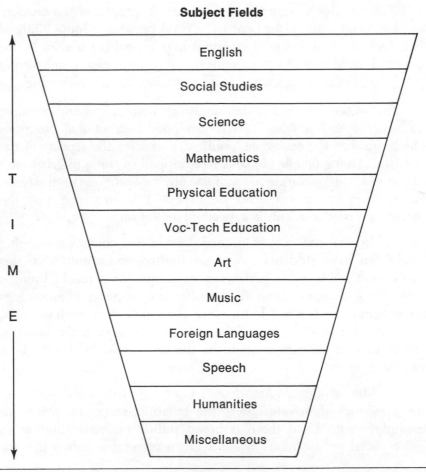

Figure 1: *Approximate time spent in various subject fields by most 14-18 year olds.*

in Viet Nam. If the "aging vat" criticism is even partially true, is there any hope for changing this situation?

Toward a Purposeful Curriculum Organization

Some observers have held that the major movements in education such as curriculum reform, innovation, and accountability have focused more on form than function. Actually a traditional subject matter curriculum can be perpetuated whether by team teaching or by an individual teacher. We must stop avoiding the question as to what schools are for and design a curriculum pattern which compels attention to those fundamental purposes that are important to students and essential to society.

It is fashionable to assign labels or acronyms to new or proposed programs. This tendency is avoided here by simply suggesting a curriculum organized around five clusters or study areas—(a) learning skills, (b) health, physical education, and leisure, (c) career education, (d) cultural studies, and (e) societal studies. An approximation of time allocation considerations for each cluster is depicted in Figure 2.

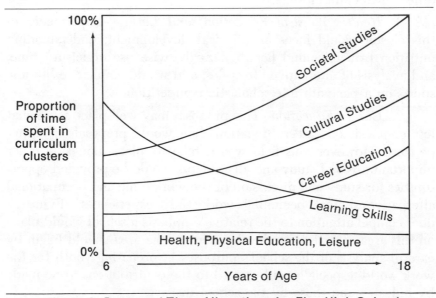

Figure 2: *Proposed Time Allocations for Five High School Curriculum Clusters.*

This proposal assumes that there are common learnings necessary for all citizens in a democratic society, and that the time emphasis must shift as students get older. The alternative school movement is, in the opinion of the writer, a healthy one since it is facilitating needed changes in the schools. However, this movement begs the question, for example, as to what the school's role shall be in transmitting the cultural heritage of the Western world. According to the proposal, as students progress toward the upper grades, a decreasing amount of time at the secondary level will be spent on learning skills. Conversely, increasing amounts of time would be spent in cultural studies. It is here that more extensive use of the community at large should be undertaken as repeatedly recommended in the proposals for reforming high schools.

Curriculum Clusters

The five study areas proposed are the following:

1. *Learning Skills*—Mathematics, reading, listening, writing, locational skills, self reliance, independent study, problem solving, reflective thought, and group techniques—these are illustrative of the learning skills all students need to function adequately in the other curriculum clusters.

2. *Health, Physical Education, and Leisure*—Experiences in this cluster would focus on physical development, understanding nutrition principles and health hazards, wise use of leisure time, and analysis of alternative life styles, and would emphasize lifetime sports on a par with interscholastic competition.

3. *Career Education*—This proposal may well place somewhat less emphasis on career education than would proposals by other persons. However, this field would take its place alongside other important areas of study and all students would be provided opportunities for study and discussion of the work ethic and occupational alternatives before beginning work-study experiences. Figure 2 does compel attention to the relative emphasis a school would place on this area. Curriculum development in the area should begin by careful analysis of the school's purposes in preparing youth for the work world, especially with regard to the contributions to be made by industry and those by the school district.

4. *Cultural Studies*—The curriculum would utilize subjects

such as art, music, speech, ethnic studies, and the humanities to focus on the agreed upon concepts, understandings, and skills that are to be sought and that are best learned through the arts. This unified approach would place heavy emphasis on multicultural education as the vehicle for creating an understanding of cultural pluralism as one of the major goals of our society.

5. *Societal Studies*—This cluster would provide the basis for a broad citizenship education designed to improve the participation and coping skills of youth. A needs assessment process which may, for example, reveal that the community ranks citizenship fourth on a listing of goals has some initial value. Yet, such knowledge is quickly seen to have only limited value for the curriculum leader. Starting points in curriculum construction would be identification of important instructional goals related to such issues as governance, resource scarcity, population, environment, interglobal dependency, the U.S. economy, poverty, and stereotyping. Such subjects as history, science, math, government, sociology, and economics would be used to deliver a unified instructional program that would help students understand the values and the social policies that are implicit in these issues. Traditional subjects would continue to be used in each cluster, but toward the purposes established for each area rather than as separate subjects in themselves.

This proposal is certainly not new or necessarily unique. What is unique is the propitiousness of the timing. While a few decades ago was obviously not a ripe time for the social reconstructionist, today may be different. In just the past decade most Americans have experienced the symptoms which make it clear that our social and economic system is in difficulty. Whether it be a gas or oil shortage, an unbalanced checking account, or dismay at the morality of our political leadership, the signs are discouraging. Actually, the schools have always been intended to shape the society rather than simply to reflect it.

Perhaps now that ideal can become a reality. This proposal for starting curriculum construction from five curriculum clusters must start with an idea made acceptable by the accountability movement—that of clarifying instructional goals. It is much more important to think first of the schools' overall purposes before instructional goals are formulated.

It will be time-consuming to work through purposes and objectives within these curriculum clusters, yet this, in the opinion of the author, must be the starting point.

Once this beginning has been accomplished, we will realize that interdisciplinary teaching will be required. This realization will mandate considerable effort in staff development activities for teachers. However, when directed toward such ends, a device such as team teaching may well endure longer than it has to date in many schools. Other innovations in organization, technology, or curriculum will prove useful in developing a powerful instructional program in each area when they are selected to facilitate a revamped curriculum.

The curriculum clusters say nothing about learning strategies. It is quite likely that action learning programs recommended in this booklet by various groups will be useful along with other strategies. Elsewhere I have suggested that we have tended to ignore much of what has been discovered through research about teaching and learning. Application of the components of an instructional theory [2] must be an integral part of moving toward the cluster idea.

This paper has reviewed several major recommendations for improving the nation's high schools. Programs such as action learning, alternative schools, shortening the school day or the years in school can be interpreted as indications that the student population and school patrons are seeking educative paths other than the traditional high school program. It has been argued that caution should be exercised lest "trivialization" of schooling set in and that, indeed, a relevant school can be envisioned if we are able to change the high school institution significantly.

There can be little optimism for a "tinkering approach" in changing the curriculum. Yet fundamentally I believe that student, teacher, and patron support can be obtained for the revisions implied by the five curriculum clusters proposed here. One is hard pressed to justify proposals for less education or for turning large numbers of students out into the community before they are equipped with better skills and understanding of the institutions in the community than our schools now provide.

[2] See: Gordon Cawelti. "Components of an Instructional Theory." *Educational Leadership* 31 (5): 427-30; February 1974.

ASCD Publications, Spring 1976

Yearbooks

Balance in the Curriculum (610-17274)	$5.00
Education for an Open Society (610-74012)	$8.00
Education for Peace: Focus on Mankind (610-17946)	$7.50
Evaluation as Feedback and Guide (610-17700)	$6.50
Freedom, Bureaucracy, & Schooling (610-17508)	$6.50
Leadership for Improving Instruction (610-17454)	$4.00
Learning and Mental Health in the School (610-17674)	$5.00
Life Skills in School and Society (610-17786)	$5.50
A New Look at Progressive Education (610-17812)	$8.00
Perspectives on Curriculum Development 1776-1976 (610-76078)	$9.50
Schools in Search of Meaning (610-75044)	$8.50
Perceiving, Behaving, Becoming: A New Focus for Education (610-17278)	$5.00
To Nurture Humaneness: Commitment for the '70's (610-17810)	$6.00

Books and Booklets

Action Learning: Student Community Service Projects (611-74018)	$2.50
Beyond Jencks: The Myth of Equal Schooling (611-17928)	$2.00
The Changing Curriculum: Mathematics (611-17724)	$2.00
Criteria for Theories of Instruction (611-17756)	$2.00
Curricular Concerns in a Revolutionary Era (611-17852)	$6.00
Curriculum Change: Direction and Process (611-17698)	$2.00
Curriculum Materials 1974 (611-74014)	$2.00
Differentiated Staffing (611-17924)	$3.50
Discipline for Today's Children and Youth (611-17314)	$1.50
Early Childhood Education Today (611-17766)	$2.00
Educational Accountability: Beyond Behavioral Objectives (611-17856)	$2.50
Elementary School Mathematics: A Guide to Current Research (611-75056)	$5.00
Elementary School Science: A Guide to Current Research (611-17726)	$2.25
Eliminating Ethnic Bias in Instructional Materials: Comment and Bibliography (611-74020)	$3.25
Emerging Moral Dimensions in Society: Implications for Schooling (611-75052)	$3.75
Ethnic Modification of Curriculum (611-17832)	$1.00

The Humanities and the Curriculum (611-17708)	$2.00
Humanizing the Secondary School (611-17780)	$2.75
Impact of Decentralization on Curriculum: Selected Viewpoints (611-75050)	$3.75
Improving Educational Assessment & An Inventory of Measures of Affective Behavior (611-17804)	$4.50
International Dimension of Education (611-17816)	$2.25
Interpreting Language Arts Research for the Teacher (611-17846)	$4.00
Learning More About Learning (611-17310)	$2.00
Linguistics and the Classroom Teacher (611-17720)	$2.75
A Man for Tomorrow's World (611-17838)	$2.25
Middle School in the Making (611-74024)	$5.00
The Middle School We Need (611-75060)	$2.50
Needs Assessment: A Focus for Curriculum Development (611-75048)	$4.00
Observational Methods in the Classroom (611-17948)	$3.50
Open Education: Critique and Assessment (611-75054)	$4.75
Open Schools for Children (611-17916)	$3.75
Personalized Supervision (611-17680)	$1.75
Professional Supervision for Professional Teachers (611-75046)	$4.50
Removing Barriers to Humaneness in the High School (611-17848)	$2.50
Reschooling Society: A Conceptual Model (611-17950)	$2.00
The School of the Future—NOW (611-17920)	$3.75
Schools Become Accountable: A PACT Approach (611-74016)	$3.50
Social Studies for the Evolving Individual (611-17952)	$3.00
Strategy for Curriculum Change (611-17666)	$2.00
Supervision: Emerging Profession (611-17796)	$5.00
Supervision in a New Key (611-17926)	$2.50
Supervision: Perspectives and Propositions (611-17732)	$2.00
The Unstudied Curriculum: Its Impact on Children (611-17820)	$2.75
What Are the Sources of the Curriculum? (611-17522)	$1.50
Vitalizing the High School (611-74026)	$3.50
Developmental Characteristics of Children and Youth (wall chart) (611-75058)	$2.00

Discounts on quantity orders of same title to single address: 10-49 copies, 10%; 50 or more copies, 15%. Make checks or money orders payable to ASCD. Orders totaling $10.00 or less must be prepaid. Orders from institutions and businesses must be on official purchase order form. Shipping and handling charges will be added to billed purchase orders. **Please be sure to list the stock number of each publication, shown in parentheses.**

Subscription to **Educational Leadership**—$10.00 a year. ASCD Membership dues: Regular (subscription and yearbook)—$25.00 a year; Comprehensive (includes subscription and yearbook plus other books and booklets distributed during period of membership)—$35.00 a year.

Order from: **Association for Supervision and Curriculum Development Suite 1100, 1701 K Street, N.W., Washington, D.C. 20006**